INTRODUCTION

I began my Italy odyssey in 1985 as a student at Loyola University's Rome Center of Liberal Arts. Since then, I've continued to explore every region and island across the Italian peninsula and record its sublime paradoxes. But my journey really began long ago in my heart as I sought out the roots of my Italian heritage that helped shape my own personality. The result has been a series of published essays that revel in the absurd beauty of Italy, which once existed as a land of vastly diverse countries and belief systems influenced by the Romans, Greeks, Phoenicians, Arabs, French, Austrians and Spaniards.

A writer by profession, I also realized that I could compose non-verbal stories-- my photographs. Using a basic 35mm camera and natural light, I spent several years documenting the textures, colors and artfully worn landscapes of Italy. This collection highlights 50 color photographs that give Italy's stones an opportunity to reveal their emotionally penetrating poetry. From a crumbling wall adorned with a bicycle in Cremona to the Adriatic poking through an arrow slit on the Tremiti Islands, these kinetic still lifes aim to encompass the country's layered sense of history, and how the past merges unobtrusively with contemporary life.

More about composition than F-stops, shutter speeds and newfangled development techniques, these photographs unveil an Italy at once grand and fragile; staunch and farcical; mysterious and unbridled.

Benvenuti in Italia!

Lucia Mauro

Interlocking corridors simultaneously conceal and illuminate the destruction of war and the renewal of peace.

Abbey of Montecassino, 1997

Whose Belle Epoque bust peers out amid the Roman pedestals – a statesman, a patriot – in this forgotten statuary graveyard?

Lecce, 1999

Shadows from the Duomo's glistening mosaic spires pierce the façade of a humbler dwelling.

Orvieto, 1997

How many lives has this decaying stucco wall witnessed passing through its door to nowhere?

Ischia, 2003

Anonymous rebels scrawl existential nothings on an avenging angel.

Caserta, 1997

The Adriatic awaits the slings and arrows of outrageous fortune.

San Nicola – Tremiti Islands, 1999

Could the elements have chiseled out a frame to give order to the earthy desolation of a city forged from caves?

Matera, 1999

A replica, perhaps, of Christ's tomb shrouded in the buttery glow of late afternoon against an unsettling blackness.

Ravello – Amalfi Coast, 1997

Sunlight slices through medieval pillars – nearly dismembering them. But they remain standing.

Bologna, 1997

Solitary perfection...barred to the public.

Bardolino – Lake Garda, 2003

It's in those private, unexpected moments when a worn relic around the corner enlightens for no particular reason.

Macerata, 1999

A temple…or an oddly shaped gutter…reveals itself as if someone etched over it with a pencil and paper.

Grado, 2003

Lust enshrined: the house – marked with a plaque – where Ingrid Bergman and Roberto Rossellini had their "love affair."

Stromboli – Aeolian Islands, 2001

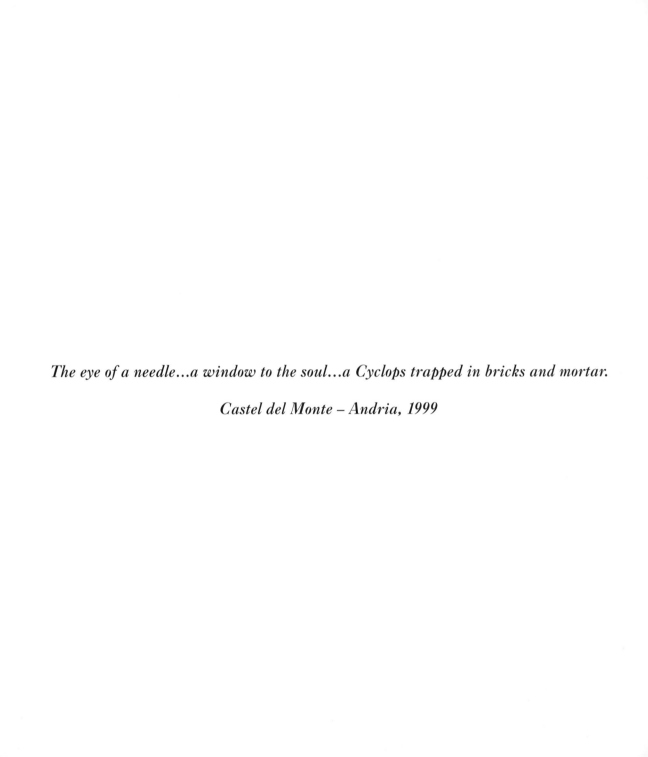

The eye of a needle…a window to the soul…a Cyclops trapped in bricks and mortar.

Castel del Monte – Andria, 1999

A ferocious wind threatened to cut loose a blood-red plastic barrier and splatter it across the pristine Medieval turrets and pure-white birch trees.

Pavia, 2002

"Rear Window" across the ages…yet the life behind them is obscured.

Bologna, 1997

Basins in bas relief, against a mustard-stained canvas.

Pavia, 2002

The Roman Empire emerges...through the foundation of a modern home...outlined in chiseled tablet form.

Cividale del Friuli, 2003

A somber athlete treads air, frozen in noble agony.

Ravello – Amalfi Coast, 1997

No amount of varnish could conceal the drama, hardship, crosses to bear…

Salò – Lake Garda, 2003

The gods play upon a pipe organ made of bone and sinew every time the hot breezes stir.

Ravello – Amalfi Coast, 1997

Lewis Carroll's mind could have ventured through this rustic looking glass.

Bardolino – Lake Garda, 2003

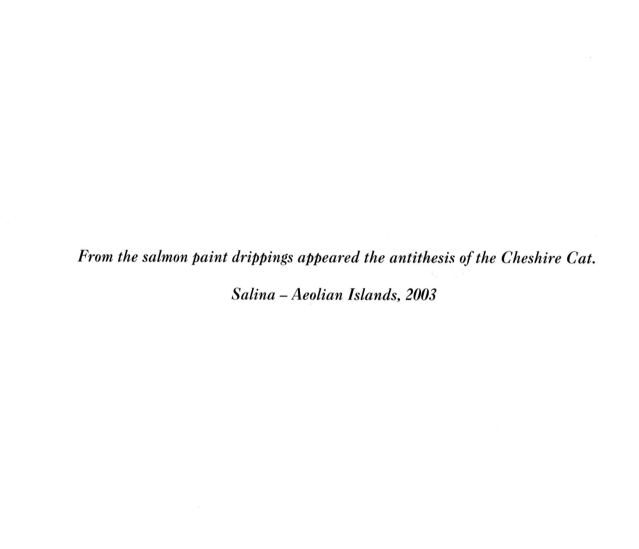

From the salmon paint drippings appeared the antithesis of the Cheshire Cat.

Salina – Aeolian Islands, 2003

A merciless sanctuary to time…

Siena, 2002

One can breathe the Age of Enlightenment as Vivaldi swirls through the chilly air.

Venice, 1999

Sacred geometry...where marble meets sky.

Abbey of Montecassino, 1997

A pigeon, caught in mid-flight, soars toward precisely aligned shelter.

Asolo, 1999

A sequestered footpath points the way to the age of train travel.

Monterosso al Mare – Cinque Terre, 2001

Barrier to entry in trompe l'oeil.

Villa Manin – Codroipo (Friuli), 2003

Uncertain celestial light beams down on a window – the result of a mathematical equation -- which completes an octagonal castle built by sorcerers.

Castel del Monte – Andria, 1999

St. Francis, in green patina, seemed to swoop from the sky to comfort an ailing dog (also in green patina).

Monterosso al Mare – Cinque Terre, 2001

Even the street name has faded into oblivion, but not wholly. One discerns the faint glimmer of mosaic stones…the only source of light on this road of caverns.

Matera, 1999

Napoleon's army, goes the legend, looted stones from Roman sarcophagi to build restraining walls.

San Nicola – Tremiti Islands, 1999

The stripes of a long-gone aristocratic clan proclaim their legacy in stone.

Bardolino – Lake Garda, 2003

Assaulted by fog and ice rain, Venice's colors ran down the cobblestone streets in trickles of black and white.

Venice, 1999

Where sepia and solitude meet.

San Lucido, Calabria – 2003

Pull up a chair...converse with the dust of entombed Etruscans.

Lipari -- Aeolian Islands, 2003

Bullet holes, bird pecks, terra cotta erosion…the pock marks of the eons.

Urbino, 1999

A dapper fellow gazes blankly into the gloom.

Trieste, 1999

A mummified Madonna blesses this street of artisans and cyclists.

Lecce, 1999

Faded patches of paint have not diminished the artistic sanctity of an old monastery on the sea.

Monterosso al Mare – Cinque Terre, 2001

Latticed prison...or homemade protection?

Macerata, 1999

I felt like I was ascending a staircase made of cotton candy.

Su Gologone – Oliena, Sardinia, 2001

And new life sprang from a rock...with fresh water as nourishment.

Desenzano del Garda – Lake Garda, 2003

How would Pablo Neruda feel about being a commodity, sold alongside crocheted handbags?

Salina – Aeolian Islands, 2003

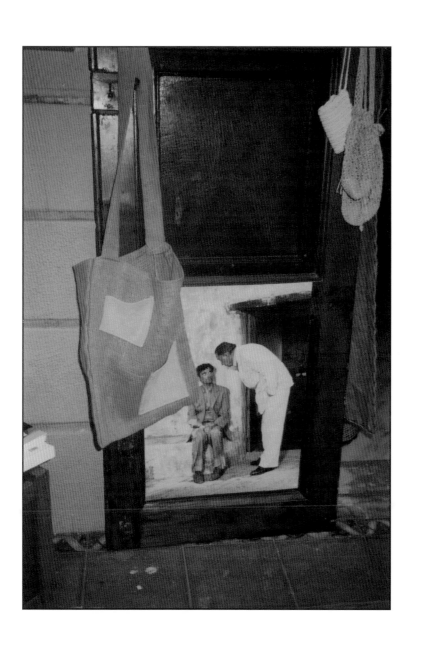

Homer's fleet sets sail...a Phoenician-infused Acropolis reigns high above.

Lipari – Aeolian Islands, 2001

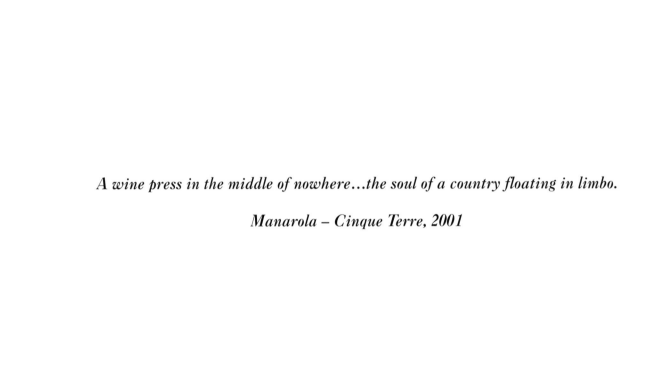

A wine press in the middle of nowhere…the soul of a country floating in limbo.

Manarola – Cinque Terre, 2001

Boats drizzled their sails into delicate water colors.

Grado, 2003

Atlantis rises again...like Botticelli's Venus.

Milan, 1995

ACKNOWLEDGMENTS

Victor, Zeferino and Cinamon Perez and Dick Westerberg at Piñata Graphics for their support

Jennifer Hansen at Piñata Graphics for her design.

Marion Color Lab for processing.

Paul Basile, editor of *Fra Noi* – national Italian-American newspaper – for the opportunity.

ABOUT THE PHOTOGRAPHER/AUTHOR

Lucia Mauro has been traveling to Italy since 1985. A Chicago resident, she publishes her personal Italy essays in *Fra Noi*, a monthly national Italian-American newspaper. Mauro i a dance critic and arts writer whose work appears in the *Chicago Tribune, Chicago Magazine, North Shore Magazine, DanceMagazine, Stage Directions* and more national arts publications She is the author of three books for McGraw-Hill, including *Careers for the Stagestruck & Oth Dramatic Types* (now in its second edition).

Mauro can be heard reading her slice-of-Chicago-life stories on WBEZ-Chicago Publi Radio, and has served as a guest arts commentator on WGN-Radio. She is frequently invited as a keynote speaker, panelist and moderator for several arts organizations, and will be fea- tured in an upcoming HMS Media documentary on "Dance in Chicago," scheduled to air on PBS-TV in the fall. Mauro also reads her creative work live in venues across the city.

This is her first book of photographs.